MINIMALISM:
Cleanse Your Life, Become A Calmer Person

By Hannah Galpin
2016

Table of Contents

ABOUT THE AUTHOR

Hannah Galpin is a writer, blogger, traveller and a reformed consumerist. She writes on the minimalist lifestyle and travel blog, **nomaderhowfar.com**, alongside her partner Taran, whilst she wanders the world living as a nomad. She has a 1st class BA in Media from the University of Portsmouth where she grew her love and passion for writing to new heights. This book is her first, but the first of many she hopes.

For Taran, who helped me become a minimalist and a calmer person, and who then helped me write about it.

INTRODUCTION: MINIMALISM AS THE CURE FOR THE CONSUMERIST ILLNESS

Is your life full of stress, worry and anxiety? Do you feel weighed down, and overwhelmed by your possessions? Are you being buried alive by your physical stuff, and then burying your head in the sand to avoid your psychological baggage? You might feel a variation of all or some of these feelings, but either way, you want to change your life, your daily routine and reach your goals, but maybe you don't have a clue where to begin with such a huge challenge.

So let's begin with a few simple questions, to help visualize a typical day.

- When you woke up this morning, did you have more than 2-3 options to choose from for your breakfast?
- As you got ready for your day, was there a few minutes spent deciding between different outfits?
- Before you were able to leave home, how many rituals did you have to complete before you could walk out the door?
- Whether you travelled to work by bus, train or car, how many of those around you were juggling luggage, various mobile devices and their morning coffee?

Before your day has gotten into full swing, you have already experienced an explosion of noise. Not literal noise, but the noise of things. The noise of having multiple options, distractions and obstacles to move through. You might find yourself stressed or impatient often, yet you have long been conditioned to appreciate having multiple options each day, for everything. Multiple choice is what our commercialised world relies upon; feeding our desire for various different versions of the same things, the agencies driving our consumption make us feel entitled to have it all, and in 5 different colours.

Having considered a typical day, and the way it plays out amidst the chaos of clutter and consumerism, you may recognize that whilst there's not really anything wrong with the things you own, you feel this inherent need to have more and more. You know that you probably have too much stuff, and you know it most likely complicates your life. And yet you can't pinpoint why you still want to keep consuming, and you see yourself as savvy to the promises made by advertisements.

It is often the case that you can be so deeply immersed in your habits and routines, that you fail to relate your problems or stresses, to your random and repetitive consumption. You are a product of your society, influenced and shaped by its capitalist values, and so your history and sense of normality, can also be your undoing. You might feel dissatisfied and unfulfilled without understanding why, or feel as if you are being constantly pulled in several directions, unable to give real authentic focus to one particular thing. In reality, you are juggling the many facets of a life you created yourself but which has also been informed by your environment. You are dropping the ball often and you sometimes feel a failure for having too much stuff, too much debt, yet too little quality time to grow and reach your goals. But you don't need to get better at managing a life bursting at the seams. Maybe, instead, you could try to lose a few balls, throwing them really far away with no intention of retrieving them. You can learn to co-exist within a society and a population embroiled in the cycle of stress, without being a victim of it. You really can have a more satisfying existence that is divorced from consumerism, the resultant clutter, and financial over-stretching; the pursuit of having it all might not be the pursuit of happiness.

Using the principles of minimalism, to tackle your problems, and become a calmer person, might just be the solution you need. But it won't be the solution for everyone...

Yes, the main topic of this book is minimalism and it suggests practical ways in which you can lead a less cluttered life, but it isn't as simplistic a text as that one word might suggest. It assists you on de-cluttering your home, changing your routines and learning to live with less things, whilst adding value to your life. It also provides advice on changing your spending habits as well as your relationship to technology. It covers a broad spectrum of issues that undoubtedly affect many people in the modern age, as merely offering the advice of cleaning out the home, would not be dealing with all of the stressful areas of life sufficiently. But it definitely doesn't posit minimalism as the solution to all problems, recognizing that life is far too complex to be defined or fixed by how much clutter we possess. We are individuals influenced throughout life by a myriad of factors, and our stress is never simply related to how tidy our home is. Our relationships, our work-life and our financial strains, all create anxiety on a regular basis, which we are often powerless but to endure.

Many people are also suffering from other deeper issues in their lives, which explains the clutter they have accumulated beyond the notion of them just being materialistic. **Psychiatrist's have stepped in to defend the causation of clutter, discussing how there is a scale of untidiness, whereby people who have the most cluttered homes are often also suffering from a bigger health problem; from attention deficit disorder, to depression, to even grief [1] .** It's comparable to a person who might go on a diet to lose weight whilst ignoring the deeper-seated reasons for their weight problem. They might regularly try different fads, and consistently fail, not because they aren't trying hard enough, but because they aren't dealing with the psychological factors underpinning their disorder.

I want to bring in an important side-note here about hoarding, which can be an underlying problem for some people. This book doesn't want to ignore nor make light of the seriousness of the condition. **Hoarding is a very serious issue, often stemming from traumatic events which lead to people keeping things that range from the useless to the down-right unsanitary [2].**

I am not a psychologist, and so I cannot safely condone the minimalist life cleanse to someone suffering from a serious mental problem which is contributing to hoarding behaviour. But to some degree, this book can help anyone on the clutter spectrum, by encouraging them to think through their problems and analyse their behaviour, even if they feel unable to implement the cleanse with immediate affect.

I feel its important to make these disclaimers upfront, because I don't want this book to shame anyone, or simplify the battles that people are fighting that this book cannot help with. But I will preface what the book can do. Whilst nothing can erase bad memories or experiences, seeing as we cannot take a magic pill to perfect the way our brains work, in order to cope with all the things that will be undeservedly thrown our way in life, we need to take back some control, which we can go some way to achieving, by first de-cluttering our slate clean.

I didn't go from a young, disillusioned graduate, depressed and in debt, to a world traveller and blogger, by just throwing things away. I tackled the parts of my life that were creating a cycle of stress, which for me was a mixture of impulse spending and the subsequent debt. I applied the principles which have become part of this book, which I then had to live out long-term, to understand the best way to show others how to use minimalism to become calmer, more organized and focused. I began this challenge two and a half years ago, by taking a hard and honest look at my situation. I decided that I had to eradicate the things that were bringing untold anxiety into my daily life. I wanted to be the person to fix the problems I had created. I wanted to take back control of where my life was headed. I decided to try and do this by cleansing my life with the principles of minimalism, and it was like an awakening. I not only discovered how my current lifestyle choices were the cause of the majority of my own personal struggles, I also realized that I had the power to change things, and that it wasn't a difficult process to start, even if it was difficult along the way.

Put simply, I tackled these 5 key area's: I cleared my debts, I decluttered my home, I simplified my online practises, I tightened my spending belt and then I started paying attention to the mindset and thought processes that were underpinning the mess I had created of my own life. The life cleanse therefore is a process and a step-by-step challenge, that in a few pages, gives you the space to rethink your life, and the tools to take back control, by applying minimalism to those 5 key areas of *your* life.

On my journey, I certainly had days where I found it really tough, where I wanted to consume. I wanted to follow my usual short-cuts to happiness and comfort by buying stuff. But I did eventually adapt to the changes, once I began to see the fruits of my labours, like the day I could say out loud that my debts were gone forever. And there were the smaller victories too, such as the result of de-cluttering my home, where I created a minimal and calming bedroom to enjoy at the end of each day.

Having come out the other side of embracing minimalism wholeheartedly, I now truly believe that our overwhelming surroundings are the key thing which distances us from being our calmest, happiest and most free selves.

This book won't debate the ins and out's of the future, be it a minimalist or materialist one. It is a practical guide for your own use, to help you channel some mindful focus to your own minimalist future. Minimalism isn't rocket science but neither are many concepts put out there in print designed to change your life for the better e.g. dieting books. People sometimes need to follow a particular text which resonates with them, and brings them on a journey of actionable steps. This book is designed to make people think deeper about their lives, whilst considering simplifying and de-cluttering as a satisfying way to make lasting change.

A minimalist future, a world where consumerism isn't the only language of success, might never be a dominant ideology. But this book focuses on the now, and how you can use minimalism right away, to get more out of life in the future. Not all that I prescribe here will work for every set of problems or scenarios you are experiencing. That's why the minimalism cleanse is an active and varied process, one you can build into your life and your thinking, but that can be introduced even in small ways.

It is a varied book in terms of chapters, and yet the final title was decided based on the reality of how you can use minimalist principles to not just become more organized, but to become calmer at your core. It takes an exhaustive approach considering a myriad of angles on the different aspects of your life, so you might think it will be an exhausting process. But the overall goal, after working through all the chapters at your own pace, is to get to a better place in your mind. If you aren't yet convinced of how minimalism and achieving calm are intrinsically linked, then consider why being a calmer person might be appealing, even if you don't believe minimalism can help you get there.

Calm is the opposite of stress, and can be viewed as a positive, relaxed state of mind or a direct reaction to a tranquil environment or scenario. Achieving calm moments each day can re-energize us, re-focus us and provide much-needed respite from the overstimulating nature of our world and our lives. But being a calm person can be also associated with a multiplicity of personal, health and social benefits. A calm person is good in a crisis, easy to approach and often easy to get along with. A calm person emanates a positive yet humble inner strength, often rubbing off on others who need their calming influence. A calm person is also likely to be healthier, experiencing less of the physiological symptoms stress can bring. Put simply, being calm feels good, and in reality, that's because it is good for you. A calm person who has simplified their life to the point of reducing the potential for further stress, is surely going to be a happier person, maybe someone who gets up in the morning eager to live out that day to its fullest potential. A calm person is somebody others can learn from, and enjoy being around. The case for becoming a calmer person is strong and so too is the case for becoming a minimalist.

A minimalist generally has less stuff, less inclination to acquire, thus less desire to spend money, and in turn, less focus on giving all their time to the pursuit of riches and 'things'. A minimalist can quite easily also be a calmer person, with less financial burdens, pressures and a general disassociation from the damaging drive of consumerism, which can be bad for your physical and mental health, let alone your bank account. **A Princeton University study from 2011 investigated how a cluttered environment impacted a person's ability to focus and concentrate, and found that it did indeed negatively affect the brains ability to work properly [3].** So it wouldn't be a stretch to say that clutter literally impacts how you perceive, understand and interact with your environment, which can then negatively effect your life and your goals.

This book posits that achieving calm needn't be a momentary thing, and argues that it can actually become your dominant state, not just a feeling reserved for the quiet occasions you can set aside to meditate, or do whatever you do to feel relaxed. Being calm can be at the core of how you approach your life, and can aid you in dealing with the unpredictable situations it will put your way. But to achieve a state of being where you feel calm and resilient in a crisis, or just peaceful enough to appreciate all the small moments which make up a good day, you first have to make changes to the way things are.

You will be invited to simplify your life, deal with the problematic aspects and alter your habits. You will join legions of others who have found value in the minimalist movement. If you are still not convinced by the theme of this book, maybe you are simply not convinced by the author.

I am hopeful that through reading this book you will draw value from it in spite of your initial scepticism. I have overcome many challenges via these minimalist concepts and it lead me to where I am today. I left England in 2015, my home, to travel the world full-time, and I now produce a travel blog with my partner, which I really enjoy. Blogging is not exactly requiring of any formal qualifications, in fact plenty of people have criticized the way bloggers impart advice as if they have some divine understanding or insight that the average Joe does not. Whilst I would never want to come from a place of condescension, and would take moves to avoid this in my writing, I do believe that it's my right to talk about my life with relatable honesty, and most importantly, share the things I have done which have helped make it more meaningful, if I believe it could help others.

The second reason I am voicing these thoughts on how to live your life, is because apparently I have helped people before, or so they've told me. Somehow amongst my bossiness and deep aversion to clutter and mess, I have translated it into useful effort which positively impacted another person. But you may still wonder, what really qualifies me to impart advice and actually believe in the effectiveness of their principles?

My real, on-paper qualifications are as follows: an honour's degree in Media Studies, some pre-University study of psychology, media and business, plus a generally studious academic life during my teen years. I lived in Southern England, a nice part of the country, but with a real contrast of affluence and poverty. As a girl growing up in a one-parent house-hold with two older brothers, I lived in nice homes, thanks to a dad who saw that we didn't struggle after divorcing my mum. We had a house full of food, and every year we had holidays abroad, although we didn't have the most harmonious of families.

I am well aware that my life has been relatively easy, from the get-go, due to my privileged position. Yet whilst I might have been born into a middle-class family, and not been subject to real poverty, or even anything resembling it, I definitely had my own special kind of bumpy ride growing up. I actually found that wealth and money confused me, in that despite its abundance, nobody in my close circle seemed overly happy, or fulfilled, as a result of their relative financial comfort. In fact, they seemed troubled, disillusioned and stressed.

I took on much of the difficulty around me, and had some struggles during school. I felt like I didn't fit in, in so many ways, and I had a hard time of it. Each day or week had some amount of bullying, which whilst common, it felt like I was the only person in the world in that much pain. This made me feel quite isolated for a time and I sought escape in a few select hobbies; eating chocolate, reading, listening to music, watching films in my room, studying, and eventually, buying things.

Upon finishing college, I took a year out in which I worked and travelled, and yet, when I started university, I wasn't certain that my degree was something that could lead to a dazzling career worthy of the financial investment. Did I even want a dazzling career, the pressure that goes with it and the push for the trappings of wealth?

When I graduated in 2012 with a 1st in Media, I was thrust into the rat-race, which I didn't feel ready to be a part of. I couldn't find my feet within a specific career path or route, and so I was mostly muddling about trying to resemble a successful adult. I spent months doing unfulfilling work, until I eventually started my own business as a dog-walker which I adored. But I still had a deep-rooted and unfathomable discord with life. I really could not understand why and thus didn't know how to fix it. It probably took until the last two years for me to realize that so much of my negative mindset was the result of being part of a complex society; diverse and inspiring in many ways, but also loud, brutal and oriented around money to a maddening level. It's not enough in this world to just want to get by, and disregard the pull of money. There's nothing wrong with ambition and passion, but when it centres around only money, it can make life harder than it needs to be. The widespread pursuit of wealth at current reaches a degree of aspiration that is so far away from what's possible for the majority of people to acquire, in a safe and healthy way.

That's why it's helped me to leave a lot of that world behind and explore further afield, to find myself in places where not a single advertisement permeates the environment. I can pretend I am not part of a world that is so unbelievably unbalanced, where the richest 1% is wealthier than all the rest of us combined. **As of 2015, a study by Oxfam calculated that 62 individuals had the same wealth as 3.5 billion people [4].**

How does that make you feel? Shocked? Disgusted? Envious? Judgemental? I am some of that, and also, amused, at the fact that being in the 99% is actually favourable to me. I can't imagine my life being all about large, ridiculous numbers and figures. I would never want the pressure of spending all my living hours tied to the acquisition or maintenance of such massive wealth, all the while unable to really experience and enjoy all the simpler things in life.

To summarize, I am someone who definitely doesn't equate having a lot of money, and a lot of stuff, with having a lot of happiness, nor success, in all the ways society likes to suggest we should. I don't believe that our value as individuals, is only measurable alongside the value of our income, our house, our car or our wardrobe. We are not the sum of our material goods, or the time we give in order to pursue them. Some of us might be privileged financially, or have grown up accustomed to that, but it does not define our future, or who we are within this difficult and unequal world.

By becoming calmer, stronger, more resilient people, disentangled from the things which make this world more problematic, we can free ourselves from our personal baggage, to then become part of a wider positive solution. If we make our money via a passion that sustains us, then maybe we can use that wealth to carve out a better existence, one which serves us and those around us. We can be successful, we can work hard, but we don't have to do it all because we feel compelled to consume. We can have a nice home, and an exciting life, without having a million objects to signify this.

Discovering the power of simplifying what I have in my life, physically and mentally, I have been able to make some peace with the world around me. This process helped me see what I truly wanted to do with my life, what my strengths are and what my purpose is, and really find out what matters, free of the distraction of life's clutter.

My own sense of purpose driving this book is foremost the desire to help others. I want my readers to become people who are freer, less bound by consumerist pressures and stresses. I want *you* to appreciate that de-cluttering, adding some organization and introducing mindful spending are achievable notions, and do simplify life in the long-run. I would love for *you* to experience the same calming benefit that minimalism has had upon me.

Whomever is reading this might be interested in minimalism, in the concept of creating a simpler life, one more ordered and organized. You might be seeking a helpful guide on how to clean out your home. You might want a little encouragement with fixing your spending habits. You might just like the idea of a refresh of the different areas of your life. Whatever your reason was for purchasing this book, I hope that you will take the time to read it, and be inspired, igniting a fresh verve for life.

The changes will come from you, but maybe the words within this book will kick a part of you into action.

This is where the cleanse steps in. I want to now begin to help you gain the clarity and freedom that I have, using minimalism to simply my life.

PART 1:1
WE ARE LIVING IN A MATERIAL WORLD

We are inhabitants of a hectic and over-populated planet, some parts horrendously poor, and completely undeveloped, however there are still millions upon millions of people living in relative luxury. Many live in comfort with the ability to have what they want, when they want. Most of them follow a certain life path, guided toward financial security and material wealth; we are born, we are educated, we learn, we study, we grow, we work, we achieve, we earn, and most importantly, we spend.

It has always been innate within society for people to strive for better, and seek out more of what we want and what we need. It's the characteristic of our evolution as a species. But that drive has changed shape over time. Now, we have departed from the beginnings of our evolution and we don't need to fight quite so hard to have an easy life. This vast improvement in general living standards over recent decades is massively related to capitalism and consumerism. **Steve Taylor PhD refutes the idea that acquiring things is a natural drive however, arguing that early hunter-gatherers naturally didn't keep things due to their nomadic ways; "...this desire would have been disastrous for early human beings" [5].**

So it would seem at some point we evolved beyond simply trying to survive; we succeeded in living beyond the basics of having food and shelter, and we now confuse our natural drives, with the ones created by capitalism. We believe that we need more than we ever did before to achieve even basic standards of satisfaction.

Abraham Maslow, a pioneer in the field of humanistic psychology, published his theory, the Hierarchy of Needs, in 1943, which purports the 5 phases of what motivates humans [6]. The first stages relate to meeting basic survival needs and this graduates to the dizzy heights of ambition in the final stage, which is about building our esteem needs, our desire for acceptance from others and a sense of prestige. This final stage is called self-actualization, whereby we reach self-fulfilment and personal potential. Maslow notes that this stage is difficult to reach for most people, and I'd argue even more so within a capitalist society, which equates our ability to make money, spend money and acquire things, with our sense of self-worth.

We are part of a world where many still live on the lower rungs of Maslow's needs, and fight to survive each day. And then there's the rest of us, our basic needs met, we want to live on the higher rungs, and often equate this with financial progress. Not everyone's goal in life is to make lots of money via their career, but even those of us who's goal might be to eventually have a family, or a home, our desires are going to be linked somewhere to money and acquiring stuff. Most of our goals come with financial commitment, so no matter what life path we follow, be it career-driven, or family-oriented, we will get caught up in the materialist consumerist dynamic which our society facilitates.

Its unsurprising that we have a widespread mindset of consumerism, being that our society was born out of the war-torn years, rife with struggle and depravation. Post-conflict, after a time of class-wide and world-wide austerity, the world entered a more prosperous state. Over time people went from needing to live in a basic way out of necessity to then feeling empowered to accumulate. And so in today's society, people rarely strive to merely live, they strive to afford a life they feel entitled too, a life their ancestors fought to build for us.

We are made to feel that not only is consumption a positive thing, a pillar of the economy, and a fun way to spend your time, but it is also your right; the right to have everything you want and desire because you are part of a world that is abundant in self-actualization. It's kind of like the American Dream ideal,but with a global and all-encompassing reach [7].

The energy behind the formation of our commercialized society was possible because of a growing and prosperous western world. The purchasing power of the general public has increased across the decades and people now aspire to have all the new gadgets and goodies on offer. When they don't have the funds to acquire things right away, they climb the corporate ladder to get them, or they enter into debt, quickly and easily, to have the markers of wealth that everyone around them has.

Money is not about paying the bills or making ends meet, and it is more than just a means to live; its a key to a world of luxury, and many of us want a copy. Maybe this is an oversimplification, and it isn't possible to explain away the human drive to consume as purely a marker of capitalist society. As I previously said, it is innate within us to strive for more because of our human instincts. We seek to be like our peers and in doing so we join them on the consumerist path. Some of us might consider ourselves to be unaffected by this human need to conform, believing that we are less obsessed with money and luxuries, and are more humble in our wants. But we are all embroiled in this way of living, some of us in subtle ways, some in more obvious ones.

There are some arguments amongst social science which don't see society as quite so black and white. **Maslow's hierarchy of needs has been discussed and expanded on by social scientist Ronald Inglehart who published a theory of post-materialism in 1977 [8].** He outlined the view that a cultural shift was seeing the younger generation, whom had grown up in the post-war period of economic security, as more likely to have values linked to environmental causes and gender equality, among other important topics; economic accumulation for the sake of it is less of a priority within this mindset. But Inglehart viewed this shift as occurring among those who had financial stability already, and had only ever known it. Thus in modern day society, we have a mixed situation; there's those who still follow the mindset of materialism to the nth degree, those who claw out of meagre beginnings to make big bucks, and then there are those who rest at the 4th and 5th phase of Maslow's needs, but are seeking self-fulfilment through something other than accumulation.

Materialism still very much exists, but it's just not as clear-cut as it once was. Improving, growing, and enlarging all different aspects of your life, from your car, to your home, to your family, remains a mindset favoured by a vast section of society. Our progress and successes are judged by ourselves and our peers, and we are often graded by our ability to expand on what we have. Minimalism might argue that this societal norm is what's wrong with the world and why it is marching headlong into trouble. It might argue that Inglehart's post-materialist world is coming forth but remains secondary, and so we will remain caught up in the negative aspects of commercialized society for a while longer.

We can appreciate that modern western society has been shaped by its suffering through a depression and a war, and thankfully, it was able to regroup, financially stabilize and prosper. So today we have a situation where financial progress is a desire within everyone on some level because for a few generations, the world truly felt the pain of poverty. Being thrifty was not a choice, it was the only way to survive, whereas today, many of us never consider thrift, because our world is great at providing us with shiny new solutions to all of our problems; all we need to do is hand over our plastic and we have a short-cut to happiness. A lot of our current society has been informed, on some level, by the depression and the war, however its the 50's and 60's where this shift really took hold.

This period brought forward the time of the 'Mad Men' with advertising able to translate into big bucks, for big business: **"It was a transitional moment in history... we became citizens last and consumers first. Ad men cut the fat on copy to make it about an emotional reaction to the product. Now, sometimes you don't even realize you're looking at an ad because it's like looking at a work of art" [9]**. Advertising grew in power as it used human psychology in order to encourage impulsive and aspirational spending habits. It used what was already within us to change the way the world worked.

In the 1980's, with the widespread popularity of cable and satellite television, advertising was further bolstered, with TV networks becoming widely privately owned and supported purely by ad's [10]. Thanks to this newly established union of vast financial strength, it was time to promote the consumerist drive, to everyone, from the rich to the poor, to those aspiring to be the rich. Of course, aspiration is the key ingredient of a receptive consumer audience. Advertising on television brought thousands of products and gadgets into the home and the family, meaning children were growing up constantly bombarded with encouragement to consume. Their parents were not exempt from the powerful influence of advertising, themselves choosing their careers and planning their lives around the acquisition of things. Be it a bigger house, a better car, or even just nicer clothes, consumers were being told that it was normality and also expected, that we all partake in the process of consistent aspirational spending.

The scope of consumerism has changed more recently, all because of our changing technology, the broader provision of choice, and of course, the internet. Consumers have the beauty of being able to buy everything they can possibly imagine, right from their desk at work or from their smart-phone. Never has it been so easy to acquire things, without really considering the choice we are making, or whether we need the item or not. Consumerism now requires less effort, concentration and less time spent wandering busy shops on the high street; this results in mindless consumption and minimal spending guilt.

The ability of the millions of people in the developed world to partake in consumerism has faltered along the way in the face of economic downturn, retreating somewhat, but never leaving. These terrible economic times have hit the rich, the poor and all in-between. But still the push to have and acquire continues, with people's purchasing power becoming the measure of how well the economy is recovering.

The economy might now be on a more even keel, which seems to help everyone sleep better at night. Once more corporations are watching the numbers rise, as we continue to line the pockets of those who want us to spend, spend, spend. But as evidenced by recent financial downturns, a reliance on the spending power of regular people is not sustainable. Our world in its current state, is not sustainable, literally. Faltering under constant demand for its natural resources combined with the mountains of landfill, our world is resembling a rubbish tip, and it might sound harsh, but in keeping with the analogy, we are the rats living within it. We mindlessly consume, never truly considering where all those things go that we discard in favour of the new and trendy. We are drowning in problems created by consumerism, and we are aware of our contribution to waste and yet also, too embroiled in it to enact real significant change, at least not in large numbers and not enough to affect the status quo.

However, some people have benefited from the financial crisis in that they have changed their spending habits to benefit themselves, and the world, in the long-run. They no longer want to work all the hours of the week endlessly if the money it brings them doesn't lead to happiness. They also don't want to give away their hard-earned money to things that are building on the worlds environmental problems. These people tend to have different interests to that of a materialist on the whole.

Its possible that those of us who have grown up in fraught socio-economic times are more likely to revert to the lower rungs of Maslow's needs. Many of us don't see it as merely surviving, we see it as a return to simplistic values that centre around what matters on a smaller, more day-to-day scale: family, having nutritious food to eat, enjoying every moment, and every morsel, as if we didn't know when we next would. The most basic of our needs can be the most fulfilling and important when we nurture them, helping us reach self-actualization, without incurring a high cost to our time, our wallets and our lives.

PART 1:2
THE FUTURE OF MINIMALISM, AND YOU

Minimalism is the antithesis of capitalism, but still, our commercialised world will try to commodify it, and is doing so already to a degree. It's hard for people of influence to argue with the power of minimalism; it worries them because of what it means for the economy. They will look to answer, where is there money to be made in the untying of peoples consciousness from the drive to consume?

Savvy opportunists, primed to build a new wave of capitalism, will endeavour to turn something as pure as a movement toward a simpler life, into a money-making scheme. You could for example accuse me of being an opportunist, jumping on a bandwagon. You are buying this book, so I am making a living out of minimalism. But there's no intention within minimalism, or this book, to encourage you to add anything other than value to your life. It's a one-off investment in yourself. Once you have simplified your life and achieved a calmer state of being, minimalism won't send you an invoice. It's a set of practises designed to untangle you from the consumerist web, not complicate your life any further.

Excessive consumption might have been your norm for as long as you can remember, but you, and the world, are waking up to the damage materialism is causing. It is not only responsible for some of your own stress and worry, but it actually threatens everybody's future. In taking on this challenge you will be questioning your place within our commercial world, your relationship to the status quo and what role you can play in changing things; for you, and society on the whole.

Authentic minimalism is about finding new, healthier ways of having and using our things, detached from stress and financial repercussions. No realistic minimalism book would ever say that we must spend nothing, keep nothing and live in an empty space, spend all our hours meditating, ignoring the outside world as it demands our attention. But the process of simplifying does have to be somewhat aggressive and extreme in order to enact lasting positive change. Reality itself is harsh but so much of our reality is created by ourselves. We are spending too much, consuming too much, and tying pure emotions to items and activities of no real significance. We retain everything from our pasts and we are terrified of the future, and so, yes, minimalism will be a radical change, and you will have to let go of a lot of literal and emotional baggage, if you want to separate yourself from the negative implications of materialist consumption.

PART 2:1
WHERE YOU ARE, AND WHAT YOU WANT

Each day we pass through a number of routines, and experience a myriad of emotions, as numerous thoughts bounce through our minds. Every now and then big events occur which stir up the pot, some good, some bad. But many of us are bored in our routines, or feel zapped of energy. Many of us are confused and tired of our emotions, and we are badgered by thoughts that never cease. We are complex, our lives are complex and everything can feel so heavy we wonder how much more we can withstand. But we don't have to feel this way forever. Our habits can change, our behaviour can alter and our viewpoint can become clearer.

You purchased this book for a reason; something about the title and the implication that it could empower you to become a calmer person, spoke to you. You must be seeking a change in your life, maybe big, maybe small. Either way, you must try and go into this process with full awareness, from the out-set, of what you hope to achieve. Its important therefore to gauge your current mood, understand the stressors in your life and the issues which have driven you toward the cleanse. This will be an important piece of material to return to if you feel de-motivated. It will also help you feel energized and excited to begin.

Take a quiet moment, get a note-pad and pen. Have a seat, and spend some time considering the following 6 questions:

1. What have been your dominant daily emotions lately? Would you say, mostly happy, mostly stressed or too busy to even stop and feel?
2. Are your most common feelings negative, or positive?
3. What do you perceive as the triggers within your life that are making you happy/sad/stressed/overwhelmed?
4. What are the aspects of your life that you believe need addressing to fix your problems?
5. What are your personal goals for the next year?
6. Why do you believe you have decided to embark on the minimalist life cleanse at this time?

These 6 questions are important because they force you to pause, and really listen to what your mind and body are telling you. Analysing how you feel, understanding why you feel it and considering the possible solutions there might be, puts you in the right mindset for big change. Its vital to take time to really focus on yourself and the direction your life is going, versus the direction you want it to go. Only when you consider in a serious and accountable manner, why you are taking on a particular challenge, can you actually make something like the life cleanse, a true priority.

Put this piece of paper to one side, somewhere it won't constantly burden you, but can be returned to when you need to.

Now it's time to move to the next phase, where we will do some deeper and honest analysis, and then take some decisive actions to de-clutter your home.

PART 2:2
BEGINNING THE CLEANSE: THE CHANGE STARTS AT HOME

The bottom line of minimalism is living with less stuff, not living *without*. De-cluttering isn't a process void of emotion or consideration for sentimentality, which is why it is integral to at first understand your own personal relationship to minimalism versus consumerism. We will do this by analysing the way you acquire things, and how you hold onto them.

Get that note-pad and pen again, and consider the following questions:

YOUR APPROACH TO SPENDING:

1. Are you an impulse buyer?
   - Do you buy something every time you leave the house?
   - Do you buy things you don't have any need for but were just attracted to?
   - Do the items near the checkout counter always grab your interest?
   - Do you regularly enter a shop without a list, and end up filling your basket with the half-price and 2 for 1 deals?
2. Are you a bulk buyer?
   - Do you over-buy when you shop for everyday items, ignoring the things needing using up at home?
   - Do you end up with a cupboard full of food, most of which has been there for months?
   - Do you buy so much of the same thing that you use it up at a more wasteful rate because you have a replacement ready?

3. Are you an emotional buyer?

- Do you make trips to the shops or shop online when you feel down, or conversely, as a reward on payday?
- Do you use spending as a cure for boredom or to find escapism?
- Do you spend more flippantly than you normally would when you feel stressed?

You may encompass all, or some of these common qualities within your spending behaviour. The traps set by advertisers might catch you, but you give into them willingly at times, satisfying an urge to spend and have something new.

YOUR ATTACHMENT TO YOUR STUFF:

1. Do you keep almost everything that enters your home?
2. Do you end up ignoring certain items or forget you even have them? Be it the irrelevant or the more valuable, from junk mail, to plastic shopping bags, from books to gadgets.
3. Does everything have its place, or do things amass in cluttered piles on surfaces, showing an unwillingness to throw things away?
4. Do you notice the piles of mess but decide that you will deal with them at a later date?
5. Do objects that might seem like mess or junk to others who visit your home, hold some meaning and relevance to you?
6. Do you hold onto things because they remind you of some past event despite being an item of poor quality?
7. When you clean your home and do your chores, do you take that opportunity to refine what you own or do you simply rearrange it?

We often have a home filled with items that we are keeping for some imagined future use, which provide no value in the present. We believe we are being thrifty, when in reality, it is simply hoarding on a smaller scale. The most useful things we have in our lives can often be counted on one hand.

YOUR ATTITUDE TOWARDS CLUTTER:

1. Are you apathetic to the mass of things in your home, with them barely registering your attention?
2. Do you feel stressed by your surroundings, where all the highs and lows of your life are represented through clutter?
3. Are you choosing to ignore the feelings that your clutter incites, out of fear?
4. Do you believe your clutter is an important part of who you are, providing tangible proof of your life?
5. If your home burnt down tomorrow, would all the important stuff that makes up a meaningful life still exist?

Hopefully these questions will have helped you to analyse, honestly and truthfully, your relationship with your stuff. You have confronted the fact that several dominant habits contribute to your clutter, to your empty bank account, to your debts, and to your over-flowing home. Now you are ready to exact some immediate change and really alter the course of your life.

I might currently be without a base, travelling and working across the world, no bed to call my own, but most of us have a place in which we inhabit for long stretches of our lives, and this place, we call home. It's where we can be ourselves, and where we can escape from the stresses of work and the general buzz of the ever busy world outside our windows. So it makes sense that it is the first aspect that needs de-cluttering attention.

Some people have the reinvigorating pleasure of living beside a beach. I was lucky enough to grow up in a city that was also close to the ocean, and I just love the feeling I get living nearby a sea-breeze and a glinting blue vista. When I'm in the kind of environment it makes me feel free, closer to nature and clearer minded. In fact all my good ideas happen whilst at the beach, but some of us have less access to the surroundings that we believe make us happy. We cannot always dictate whether we live in a small village in the country, a house looking out to sea, or a buzzing concrete jungle. But if you cannot drastically alter the world outside your window, you can still carve out a place that makes you feel happy behind that window.

Your home should be a space that visually compliments and stimulates your hopes, your dreams, and your goals.

It is possible to create a life where you pursue new hobbies for more than just a week, your home no longer collecting miscellaneous items detailing your short-lived efforts at various things. It makes sense that we don't add to our stress by filling our space up to the brim with stuff that only make us feel inferior, tired or frustrated.

A minimalist home needn't be an empty one, void of individuality, inspiration or interest. It might be a tidy and organized place, cultivating calm, but it can also feed our wonders and our passions. Some minimalism projects can go wrong when people reduce their material footprint so thoroughly that they end up stripping too much away, and their home becomes an empty shell. We don't want to live our lives as empty shells; we want to be challenged, fulfilled, excited yet balanced, and so our homes should help us do this.

Let's begin, with the 3 step process to changing the way your home looks, works and feels. The key idea I want you to take through this process is that it must be a mindful and honest analysis; you will approach de-cluttering with those three ideas at the core.

This de-cluttering framework can be applied to every room in your home because its based on measuring each individual items usefulness and relevance secondary to evaluating how much you own of each item type; from having multiple grey t-shirts to sort through, to having 5 different styles of crockery, you will assess which of these are the most logical to keep, as well as considering item quality, usefulness and sentimentality.

This is an efficient method because you will be generally reducing how much you own of each item type, instead of working toward having a specific and fixed number of each item type. For example, you aren't working toward having 1 winter jacket , or 1 decorative trinket, or just 1 mixing bowl, instead, you are reducing the general volume of what you own on the whole.

There will certainly be space for keeping the things you enjoy or love, items which can't be defined as integral to your very survival. By letting go of your least useful items, multiples, duplicates and other random junk, thus creating a generally less cluttered home, you can then bring your most beloved things to the forefront of what you see and experience each day.

26

STEP 1:
REVIEW AND REMOVE.

1. Pick the smallest room or space in your home. By starting small you can build up to the bigger challenges by achieving quicker successes first.
2. Start with one surface, box, shelf or cupboard. Whatever is calling out to you as the most obvious place to begin, start there.
3. Pick up the first item you see.

- Is the item something you use every day?
- If not, do you use it once a week?
- When did you last use it, and do you see yourself using it again soon.
- Consider if you have a similar or superior version of the item that you could keep and use instead.
- If you have the tendency to keep an item based on some imagined future use or need for it, consider how long you have had the item, and whether it has been useful thus far.
- If the item has not been used recently, and probably won't be used again, consider if it has sentimentality.
- Is the item useful, but nonetheless no longer useful to you.
- If the item was cheap, easily replaceable, or has been in your home for a long time, and not used at all, then its future purpose is less important.
- If the item is determined to be no longer useful to you, an inferior version of something else you own, nor sentimental and beloved, then discard this item.

All the items that you remove, place in boxes, or bags, with the view to either DONATE, TRASH or SELL.

Try to immediately remove these boxes from your home which you can do by designating a day in which you take all your clutter to its new homes. That day will be when you say goodbye to your stuff, but hello to your new space, so you must embrace the process of removing it all swiftly, letting go of the burden of it from your life forever.

KEY RULES FOR REMOVING ITEMS:

- Don't make a decision about an item, move it, and simply forget about it. Place it in the designated box or bag for removal.

- Much of what you discard will be something someone else might want, but sometimes it will just be rubbish. Don't give your junk to someone else, to become their junk.

- Some people hate being wasteful, and yet do not make the connection between acquiring things and the eventual guilt of discarding them. You will have to set aside your avoidance of throwing things in the trash, by doing this big de-clutter once, and then promising that this will be the last time you have to do such a major purge.

- The reviewing and removing phase should not be a two or three part strategy; if possible it is best to set aside time in which you can review, discard and immediately remove from the home. If not, you will just find yourself holding onto things and delaying the inevitable.

- When setting aside time to review, remove and discard, all in one day, you could assign a room or a set of rooms to these particular days. For example, set aside a Saturday to de-clutter your lounge, box it all up and remove it that day. Don't try to de-clutter every space in one time period, as this is entirely unrealistic and highly stressful. If however you naturally move from one room to the next, and you de-clutter more than you initially planned to, then that's a positive thing, but try to assign an initial goal for a particular day instead of taking on too much.

STEP 2:
MAKE PEACE AND LET GO

Each item which you can't immediately discard, must hold some significance in your mind. I want to really discourage getting rid of sentimental items on a whim, because whilst you can certainly overthink something and talk yourself out of discarding, you do need to give attention to that niggling reluctance and really try to analyse it.

As I previously said, no minimalist home should be devoid of personality or not representative of our lives, but sometimes letting go of certain items helps us make peace with painful memories. Sometimes we view the detrimental, as the sentimental, and that's what this process helps you decipher. When we confuse items in this way, we are somewhat held back by the hold of that item. Not only are we surrounding ourselves with daily reminders of events that we could could move on from, but this also further encourages an emotional relationship with acquiring and keeping things, which over time, leads to clutter, and then stress.

1. Place each of the sentimental items in front of you, one-by-one, and give yourself 15-30 seconds with each item.

- In that 15-30 seconds, allow your natural thoughts to process, and see what feeling this item gives you.
- What words or emotions immediately spring to mind? Listen to what that item is, instead of just looking at it.
- In that time-frame it should be obvious whether this item is merely a partial remnant of a memory, or a significant artefact from your life-story, one to be cherished and given pride of place.
- At the end of the 15-30 seconds you *must* decide to discard or keep the item.
- If however you are struggling to conclude what to do with some items, ask yourself when you last looked at the item and enjoyed it.
- Is it tied to an unhappy time, or a memory you are unable to let go of?
- Does it represent a major life event to you?

- Consider that no item can summarize or contain the memories which you struggle to confront or desire to hold onto.
- Recognize that no object is completely representative of you, your life, your role within your family and relationships, whether good or bad.
- Is the item actually bringing anything to your daily life?
- Can you see yourself being either the same, sadder, or being happier, if you let go of this item?

2. With each sentimental item that you absolutely refuse to let go of, put it into a medium sized box, label it KEEP, and set it aside.

- This box will be a place to store these things until you find a better way to display, enjoy and appreciate them in your home.
- It should be the main place that sentimental items are kept during the home cleanse process, and it will be returned to later.

When letting go of certain items, consider, might you be giving sentimentality to them when they aren't even that rare or special to you. No one thing is indispensable, when our most important life moments often surpass the meaning of any tangible thing.

A prop of a special memory neither adds nor takes away from the reality that you got to experience something beautiful, precious or life-changing.

Throwing away some items that you might at first never dreamt of discarding, can become an easier process when you remind yourself of that fact.

STEP 3:
RE-THINK AND RE-ZONE YOUR AREA'S

Your home really can work *for you* or *against you*, whatever your daily routine or goals are. A tidy home can work for anybody, but there is a level of effort involved in maintaining tidiness, which is why minimalism is so useful in cutting back on your cleaning routine. Step 3 of organizing and de-cluttering your home, involves a rethink of your living space.

It's time to consider, are you getting the best out of each room, and is it living up to the purpose you previously assigned to it. Is your home a space you want to be in, a place where you feel like you can work toward and live out your goals. Is it a place that can inspire, motivate, comfort, and relax you, all at the same time.

1. Sit down in each room within your home for a few minutes, and observe your natural thoughts and feelings.

- What words, phrases or ideas are popping up in your mind?
- Consider the purpose of that room. Is it working well for what you need it to?
- If the room is a sleeping space, is it conducive to a peaceful night?
- If the room is a work-space, is it free of distraction and yet not devoid of creative energy.
- Establish if that room could be better organized or arranged to meet your goal for the space.
- Experiment with the existing furnishings, removing some or moving them into different places to see how they make you feel.

2. Consider creating a room with a new vibe or purpose, one that is suited primarily to selfish goals, or that represents a hobby or passion.

- A room that is expressly for reading, or watching film's, is a nice idea, but a small home may not have the space for this. Instead, pick small pockets or corners within your home that can be transformed.
- The addition of a comfy corner chair can change the dynamic of an office-space, into a place you find cosy and comforting, as opposed to stifling.

- Removing the television from your bedroom can mean the room becomes a space for minimal visual distraction around bed-time.

3. As well as creating inspirational spaces, allocate purpose to certain areas for things such as paying bills and doing general admin.

- A disorganized person who is unable to keep up with their admin will find paperwork in 10 different places in the home, and every time they walk past those different places, it stresses them out.

- Keep all your stress-inducing paperwork in one particular zone, creating a nook where you put any documents or mail which enters your home, and don't allow it to spill over into your other spaces.

- By restricting this stuff to one small space, your home becomes organized, functional *and* more relaxing.

4. Consider making the best of your most cherished mementos and photographs by creating a memory wall or shelf, a space to display those things placed in the KEEP box earlier.

- This not only helps you to regularly reconnect with the possessions that you have chose to keep for sentimental reasons, but it reaffirms an appreciation for the quality of these things versus the irrelevant ones you discarded.

- This also discourages further consumption of meaningless, cheap and fashionable objects, which will ultimately bring nothing but clutter to your space.

STEP 4
KEEPING YOUR HOME AND YOUR LIFE ORGANIZED

At this stage you have analysed your relationship to your stuff, de-cluttered your home, created spaces which work better for you, and now you want to prevent the clutter amassing again. We will address the issues with spending in a later chapter, but first we will look at methods of maintaining your newly organized and reinvigorated space.

You probably recognize that having a cluttered home isn't simply the result of over-spending, or being sentimental, much of it is down to apathy. Not any kind of shameful slovenly attitude, but the simple fact that when we are busy, we don't have the time to do much of anything we actually want to do, let alone clean. And yet when we do have free time, we still don't use it to address our clutter even as it builds up to stressful levels, because there are other things we would rather be doing.

The following ideas will help you keep your home tidy and uncluttered but won't swallow up time from your busy life.

Firstly, for maintaining overall organizational flow in your life, you should have a diary. Not a virtual one, living entirely on your mobile phone or tablet, but a physical notebook. The one I swear by uses a weekly planning format, where I have 4 separate spaces allocated to each day.

- I use one space to write down my expenditures for that day (this means I can throw receipts away immediately).
- I use another to highlight my to-do-list (I tick off as I go).
- I use the third space to remind myself of things such as bills due that week or day (I never miss a payment and go accidentally overdrawn).
- In the 4th space I list what I did that particular day e.g. worked, went out for lunch, worked on my blog (I take note of what I achieved to help keep myself on-track with my general life goals).

I can't recommend a specific brand or diary (I got mine from a local discount store) but the concept of writing everything down has really changed my daily routine.

- I can now quickly see not only my to-do-list but go back and track my spending, see exactly what I did 2 weeks ago, and also plan ahead.
- A diary is not a new concept but it's becoming out-dated to some of us who do everything via the calendar or notes apps on our devices. Having a physical record that you have to take time to write makes you much more focused and aware of your goals and plans.
- It also allows you to stop relying on your brain to remember every single thing you believe it needs to, from what day your next phone bill is due, to when a family members birthday is.
- When you don't help yourself out by writing things down, you will end up forgetting some stuff along the way, but a diary takes away the stress of constantly juggling all your thoughts and responsibilities.

So now that you have a diary, a place to physically pigeon-hole all the important details from your daily life, you may now want ideas on how to maintain your organized home space. The steps discussed below relay a few simple rules that you can bring into your routine.

I really believe that when you stick to a few simple method's in how you manage your home, you can maintain control over it in the long-run. And so the next step brings in 3 rules that are essential to maintain your newly de-cluttered space.

1. First, is the **'Everything has a home'** rule. Every single item that comes into your space, must have a place where it belongs.
- Be it a specific drawer, cupboard or shelf, everything must be put in its place soon after entering your home.
- Maybe you designate one specific cupboard for breakfast foods, or one particular draw for mail and receipts.
- At the end of each week, you will review these 'homes' and analyse them honestly.
- You will count the quantities stored in each home, every week, for one month.

- At the end of the month you will review your findings, going back over what was originally in the newly established homes, and what remains there.
- This is not just about keeping things organized and making it easier to get to what you need quickly, but its important in other ways.
- This process forces you to notice the areas of your home which gather the clutter of life and then consider just how much stuff you are allowing to stay in your home.
- This rule can actually save you money too. For example, it might make you look harder at your food consumption, and consider if you are spending extra money adding new things when you already have enough food to eat.
- It makes you confront your stuff and what it says about you and your life. A drawer full of receipts after a week is going to give you pause for thought on your spending. A pantry shelf busting with packaged snacks might make you look at your diet.
- This rule is all about analysing your relationship to the things you acquire, to help you make better choices about what you consume.
- It also discourages waste, as you will be fully aware of just how much of something you are collecting and not using, e.g. food.

2. Alongside the rule above, you will add in a time each day where you will tidy your home. This will be your **'5 minute blitz'**.

- You set a timer, and then move room to room, at pace, putting items away into their homes, generally tidying and organizing.
- The purpose of this rule is to ensure cleaning is not a time-consuming activity. If we can deal with things in short focused bursts, then we can leave more time for valuable activities.
- It's also designed to make cleaning fun. Yes, fun. There's definite satisfaction to be found in these 5 minutes each day, which yield much appreciated results, such as having a tidy lounge to relax in each night, or a bedroom with no mess to face at bedtime.

- Just 5 minutes a day is much more doable for those who are adverse to hours spent spring-cleaning.
- This rule should cut-down on your overall cleaning regime, which makes the next rule easier to stick to...

3. Now comes the third and final rule for your newly organized space, **'The monthly refresh'**.

- Pre-plan a day in your month where you will deep clean your entire home. Use your diary to plan ahead for this.
- Set yourself a time limit for your deep clean, otherwise the idea can become mildly overwhelming, and you might dread it if you think it will take up a lot of your day.
- Your deep clean will involve cleaning all those things you regularly ignore, like the cobwebs in the corner of the ceiling, or the top of the bookshelf that collects dust.
- This is about not simply having a clean home, its about ensuring your home doesn't revert to it's pre-cleanse state.
- Its also about maintaining a pro-active attitude in response to your surroundings. You took back the power in aligning your home with your goals and desires, this can help you maintain that power.
- Planning for a monthly deep-clean allows you to relax your regime, especially as your 5 minute-blitz should maintain your home the rest of the time. Of course, you may want to clean your home more often than this, but the monthly refresh should focus on the things ignored in the 5-minute blitz, which in-turn keeps the home vastly clean, and ensures the 5-minute blitz can remain a brief but effective daily routine.

Hopefully by now you will have tackled your physical clutter, and addressed your daily and monthly routines to help prevent further mess and de-cluttering. The next chapter will focus on an entirely different area of your daily life, zeroing in on your technology use and virtual clutter...

PART 3:
TECHNOLOGY: MAKING YOUR LIFE EASIER YET HARDER

We live in a technologically advanced society, where we have access to a myriad of gadgets, all supposedly able to make our lives easier. The inference is that having certain apps on your phone or tablet provides must-have short-cuts and life hacks. The fact that we all survived just fine before their invention is a second-hand thought, left far behind amidst the bright colours and carefully constructed designs we feast our eyes upon daily. Our passion and obsession for gadgetry is also a marker of a society living with everything at close-hand, luxuries common-place and a consciousness that is taking in numerous processes, virtual and real, all happening at once.

Most of us, of all ages and budgets, have access to these rapidly changing technologies. Millions of people walk around brandishing shiny screens that they might admit to feeling lost without. Do they help us to connect with people and be organized, creating an easier life thanks to the work of smart technology, or do they actually add a confusing and frustrating middle-man to our routine?

Technology can also be distracting, and great in aiding procrastination. For many people, these gadgets make-up their daily down-time and hobbies, and are often used during the quiet or dull moments of the day. Why look out the window on the bus, or talk to people in the queue at the supermarket, when you can stare at your phone? There's a selection of apps and social networks waiting to fill your eyes and your brain with information, which you often forget the next moment. Most of it is inane and pointless and many of us would admit that we can't even recall what we just scrolled through not long after putting our devices down. And yet, endless scrolling is a common pass-time of this generation.

We have come to prefer the immersion of our gadgets over what is actually happening around us. It's not quite virtual reality, but it is a portal through which we momentarily escape our lives, but what we are actually doing is living vicariously through the lives of others. We are voyeurs, not just following and observing different points of views and lifestyles, but we are drawn in so deep, it begins to change how we think about the world. The online universe can be just as difficult, painful and problematic to navigate as the real one, but since when did joining in on the latest popular app, or watching others lives play out on social networks, supplant our investment in our own existence?

This behaviour has become habitual, and so, like other habits, it is supposedly formed out of repetition. Many habits that are repetitive and are engaged in regularly, are also known as something else; addictions. **Bill Davidow (2012) talks about the neuroscience involved in internet gaming and the concept of the compulsion loop: "...we're beginning to understand that achieving a goal or anticipating the reward of new content for completing a task can excite the neurons in the ventral tegmental area of the midbrain, which releases the neurotransmitter dopamine into the brain's pleasure centers... some people can become obsessed with these pleasure-seeking experiences and engage in compulsive behaviour such as a need to keep playing a game, constantly check email, or compulsively gamble online" [11].**

So, pleasure and internet use have become inextricably linked, but when you break it down, does half an hour looking at Facebook really bring you enjoyment? Do you associate time spent on social networks with fun and laughter? Do you feel happier once you have visited your social networks? Are you just going on these apps out of pure habit, being so disassociated from the activity that you don't even question it?

My favourite and most relaxed parts of my day, aren't those spent frowning at my screen; they are spent looking around, observing the faces of those bustling about me and listening to their various conversations. I love taking in the life actually happening around me in that present moment. The times my mind is the most pleasantly quiet is when I listen to music whilst I walk home from work, as I slowly take in my route and notice the blue of the sky against the tree palms as they blow gently in the wind. This focus on experiencing the present moment, and engaging in simpler activities, minimalist at their core, often fills me with calm. The concept of entering my own little virtual bubble simply doesn't compare to just quietly observing what's really happening around me.

When we focus on the real living world, we sometimes find ourselves more inspired, entertained and relaxed than we could ever imagine. It is not wasted time that you could be Netflix binging, its mindfulness, and there is a lot to be said for its relationship to our mental well-being. There's only so much escapism a person can do before they lose sight of how to make themselves happy without the aid of technology.

If we simplify our technology, and spend less time immersed within it, we create useful moments, where we can be doing healthier things. We can derive our pleasure from real life, not the edited, loud and overwhelming version we see online.

STEP 1:
DELETE AND UNSUBSCRIBE

This is the discarding phase of the technological cleanse, albeit you just hit a few buttons instead of physically throwing anything away.

The beauty of this phase is that the decisions you make can technically be undone and so psychologically, it should be an easier process.

1. Pick up your most used daily device. You can go through these steps on all of your devices one by one if you wish.
   - Count how many apps you have.

- Of these apps, move the ones you use every day to the home screen or first page on your device.
- Review the apps that you didn't need to move to the home-screen. Consider when you last used each app, or go into the app settings on your phone to find this information.
- Straight away delete any apps that you haven't used in the past month.
- Consider deleting ones that you recently added impulsively but haven't yet used.
- Sort your apps into folders, labelled with simple titles such as 'READ', 'WATCH', 'LISTEN'. Placing the apps into folders as opposed to just placing them individually on your home screen might make you less likely to visit the ones that commonly lead to time-wasting and endless scrolling.
- You may learn over time which apps are most addictive and that you are more likely to search through your folders to use each time.
- Review the folders once you have organized them and consider if you could still delete some apps.
- The technology we use is designed to make our lives easier, and yet a device clogged with numerous apps becomes hard to navigate. You can even forget what apps you actually have. The next part of deleting sends you to your mailbox.

2. Open your mail app.
- Click on all unread emails in all folders.
- Read and delete. If they are important or you need to keep them, create a folder related to the email subject.
- Review old emails that have been read but kept. Consider moving these or deleting them.
- If you previously took the time to field certain emails to your 'filtered' folder, it's time to actually address these. Go to the very bottom of the email content, emails which you never read or ever intend to, and hit *unsubscribe* to stop receiving them.
- Go into folders you have created in the past and look through to see what you can delete.

- Get into the habit of reading every email you receive and immediately deleting, unsubscribing or moving. Eventually you will go days without needing to read any at all as you will be receiving far less.
- In the future, if you sign up to a website or app which send out regular emails, unsubscribe from the first one you receive if it is of no real benefit to you to read.
- If you have multiple email accounts, consider deleting them and sticking to one personal, and one professional.

3. Pick up your most used device again, and look at the amount of data, be it photo's or documents, stored on these.

- Do you regularly back the important data up to a hard drive device or to cloud storage?
- If so, could you get out of the cycle of filling up the space on your devices because you never review and delete data, by backing up more often, then deleting the original data weekly.
- Create folders on your devices which house your most important information or data, and make sure all new data is saved to these folders.
- Review your photo folder or gallery each week, and complete a manual backup if you aren't already automatically backing up.
- Delete at least 20 photo's each time you review it. This is about not just having a phone that's easier to navigate but it also forces you to get more out of the photos you regularly take and never enjoy. It might even encourage you to create something special with them.

STEP 2:
UNFOLLOW AND UNLIKE

Many people of all generations now use social media daily, and some of us look at it first thing in the morning just after we open our eyes, before we have even formulated any real thoughts. Social media is addictive, and most of us can't remember what we did before it existed.

All those times we sit scrolling through our various accounts, ignoring most things, reading and 'liking' some, what did we do with all that free time before! I do think these accounts hold some value, keeping us connected with people and their lives, fostering a place for open and honest discussion, but how often do we actually use it for those purposes? Are we actually creating inner turmoil and anxiety by constantly looking through these busy and information-packed feeds?

A set of studies conducted in 2012 by Anxiety UK, made the following findings about the linkage between frequent social media use and anxiety: "Respondents who regularly use social networking sites saw their behaviour change negatively. Further investigation revealed factors such as negatively comparing themselves to others, spending too much time in front of a computer, having trouble being able to disconnect and relax, as well as becoming confrontational online, thus causing problems in their relationships or job"[12]. The study also supports the idea that our social media can be helpful and great for people confined to their homes, but still, it can have a major impact on our mental well-being.

We end up liking pages and following accounts, thus signing up to then see every update those accounts ever post. Sometimes we follow an account that's a topical thing, or a passing trend, and so over time it becomes irrelevant being on our social feed. And yet rarely do we take the time to remove these things from our feeds. We actually just ignore them, as if we are scared to cut off the connection.

In this step we will look at our social accounts and take moves to reduce the amount of things which get onto our news feeds. We will create social spaces which deliver things which are of the highest value to us, and restrict the amount of random and useless information we take in.

Open your Instagram, Facebook, Twitter, and whatever social networks you might be on, and lets do an audit...

1. Observe your immediate thoughts and reactions to each account that you regularly scroll over/read updates from.

- Is it someone or something you regularly engage with, online or in real life?
- How do the accounts updates usually make you feel?
- What brings you to look at certain accounts on a regular basis?
- If you are following an aspirational person or account, with the aim of seeking out motivation, question if these accounts bring positivity to your daily life, or negativity.
- Consider how much of your social media activity involves looking up people or topics, that you would not want to admit to searching for in real life?
- Could this be a signifier of an issue that you might be unable or afraid to discuss in real life, and so looking at these accounts satisfies curiosity, which over time can become obsessive and unhealthy.
- When we use the online world to seek out solutions to our problems or answers to our questions we don't always find the right thing for us, with it being a place full of misinformation and non-specific advice.
- Notice how many sponsored posts or advertisements you see on your various feeds. Social media might have begun as a social domain for communication but it soon became a profitable advertising space. You can't escape the pull to consume, even on your social media where you believe you have agency over what you see. Read through a feed for 5 minutes and count how many ad's you see.
- Relate this to not only your desire to consume less and acquire less clutter, but to your search for more inner calm. Is the bombarding nature of superficial advertising harmful to your plight of consuming less?

2. Observe how much of what you see is that which other people have shared, or liked, and consider how this is a constant push for you to keep clicking on articles, and keep responding to visual stimuli with your thumbs.

- A lot of what we regularly see on the internet can be referred to as 'click-bait' meaning the content producer knows what language and imagery to use to garner a few minutes of our precious attention. You might never consider just how much of your online activity is made up of hours spent giving attention to information that you never sought out in the first place.
- Observe how many invitations to click, read or share are present on your social feeds.
- Consider how many of these you feel pulled toward clicking on.
- Click on these and then view the content. Is it advertising? Is it something designed to encourage consumption, or is it an interesting and vital piece of information?
- What are the most common things you click onto? If they are very much click-bait items, consider unfollowing these accounts, as its probable that these kind of sites rarely deliver something equal of the title or worth reading.

Considering all the above ideas, click to unfollow any account which you can evidently see is bringing very little value to your social media practices.

You may have found through this exercise that you are often giving disengaged passive attention to the actual real people on your feeds, instead giving time to lots of clickbait or advertising content. You are subjecting yourself to endless random information of no real long-term use to you. You are also being tempted to consume constantly, in a way that is more sly and covert.

STEP 3:
REFINE YOUR BROWSER BOOKMARKS AND FAVOURITES

If you are a busy person who centres both your hobbies as well as your work around being online, you probably bookmark and favourite things of interest often. You most likely have many links saved in random folders on your browsers, so you either end up forgetting about valuable websites or information you want to return to, and simply end up with a very clogged favourites folder.

It's time to bring your attention to how you organize your internet browser and thus optimize your relationship with the online stuff that is of real value to you. From your social accounts to your favourite inspirational blog posts, reorganizing and deleting some favourites and bookmarks will mean you can create a less cluttered online space.

1. Look at your current bookmark folders of favourites. These will be a collection of web-pages and websites you have saved over the years.
2. Delete the links which are outdated or no longer of interest.
3. Create folders covering the topics of most importance to you and begin to save only the most relevant or favourite bookmarks to these.
4. Set a goal of reading or using these bookmarks for reference, soon after adding them, instead of forgetting about them and the very reason they were originally of interest to you.
5. Going forward, never favourite a website link or article unless you specify the folder you want to save it in, or create a related folder.
6. Resist the ease of pressing the little star button on every web-page that remotely intrigues you and then forgetting about that page forever.

STEP 4:
CREATING MEANINGFUL ONLINE ACTIVITIES

I often read numerous news or blogging posts each day that either entertain me, make me think a bit deeper about something, educate me, or simply make me laugh. But these short periods of reading valuable content then get forgotten and lost to the next article that grabs my attention. That's why I believe step 4 is the most important of all the technology steps.

This step is about acknowledging that the online world is one full of useless and empty information, but also one full of the stories and experiences of people from all walks of life, all over the world. The internet was once a primitive and limited tool, which then became utilized for communication, education, then it became about commerce, then the cult of personality and celebrity, and is today a heady mix of all those themes. But the best way we can derive value from the information overload out there is to separate the good and valuable information, from the bad.

We have already streamlined our device apps, our social media feeds and interactions, and then organized our internet browsers, but we now need to analyse a bit deeper, to understand why and how we use our technology.

1. Set a timer when you sit online, on your phone, tablet or laptop, then review how many hours you spend on them each day.
- Write down the things you remember most from your online activities; what did you actually do online?
- Did you watch something, read, learn, be creative, talk with family or friends?
- Did you surf a myriad of sites spending 2-5 minutes at a time reading random stories and news?

2. Establish how being online actually makes you feel, to consider how much of your time spent there is actually achieving something positive, in-line with your daily goals.

- What are the common emotions you feel during your online sessions?
- Are the emotions or feelings more positive, or negative?
- Can you link your current online activities to good memories or happy moments?
- Has something you read online changed your life for the better? Or has something you have read negatively impacted you?

3. Think about reducing the amount of different sites which you visit and try to find 3 core online spaces that bring you something of value.

- Be it based around your hobbies or interests, or just a place that you find inspiring content on, choose to give to your attention to a limited set of platforms, but which vary in content.
- Consider the quality of the content and the content producers on the sites you spend the most time reading.
- Could you be filling your brain with food for thought, instead of being pulled in by gossipy websites that give you useless information about people you don't know or things you don't need to know about?
- Are you learning about the world from impartial sources, or politically-motivated and sensationalist sites?
- Do your most visited platforms barrage you with covert advertising in the form of content?
- Resist the often confusing practice of visiting and scrolling several different sites a day, choosing 2-3 as your favourites from now on, to derive more positive value out of less time spent at your computer.

The focus of this section was still intensive but might have seemed trivial in comparison to the other chapters. Theoretically, you could just go on your devices less, and thus not need to refine your every online activity to such high minimalist standards. But this is a simple set of tasks which will ease you into a healthier relationship with your technology. These steps certainly will help you to see the far-reaching depth, complexity and influence, that your online interactions have on your real life.

PART 4:
MONEY COMES, MONEY GOES

By now, you have successfully de-cluttered your home space, and feel renewed by the process of simplifying your surroundings. Then, you simplified further, assessing how technology eats into your time and can starve you of your imagination and relaxation. Now it's time to address one of the underlying aspects that created a cluttered home and a smart-phone overflowing with apps: money.

You cannot truly cleanse your life without considering the role your spending habits has in the general clutter that fills your physical and mental environments. Addressing and changing your attitude to spending and saving might be the only way for the cleansing process to have long-term success.

Firstly, I'd like to bring in a bit of background about money and I. I grew up in a fairly fortunate family. My dad worked hard as my brothers and I grew up, and he created a comfortable life for us. I learnt from a young age that I was definitely privileged in comparison to some friends who hadn't yet been on a plane. Even after my parents were divorced, I have never really been in financial trouble. Financial stress is another matter; fortunate beginnings does not mean that I never worry about money nor have I not experienced financial difficulty in recent years. Travelling is probably one of the most stress-inducing life decisions, because it is a choice you make and then have to fund to continue it. Jobs aren't always easy to come by as a traveller so I have willingly entered an anxious financial situation. But a life lived in one place, with one steady job and lifestyle, is still a stressful financial prospect.

Things go wrong every day, which incur unexpected costs, ones we may or may not have prepared for. Costs which we have no choice but to pay. An unexpected cost might be a car breakdown, and if your car is integral to your life, then its not something you can avoid paying for. However an unexpected cost is never a new dress or a state of the art juicer, and yet they have a hidden cost. When we fill our lives with consumerism, and when our spending becomes mindless and often, we create a situation of excess. Not only do we end up with too many things and objects, all competing for our attention, many of which we had no need for in the first place, but we get accustomed to having enough money, to be able to waste it.

Another thing that can go wrong in our lives, and is sometimes wholly unavoidable, might be losing a job. When this happens, there is not simply the stress of finding a new job, but also the fact that you will be surrounded by objects and financial commitments that represent the value of the wealth you had, and spent. The sense of disappointment and regret that this can create is an added problem to an already worrying situation. We may have taken on financial responsibilities whilst we had the income to afford them, and yet, when that income goes, it isn't always so easy to lose those commitments too. This is even more compounded by the fact that you may not have any savings set aside, in preparation for this torrential downpour of a day.

When you live for today, and spend often, or without much thought, you neglect to think to your future, and in doing so, you create a perfect recipe for stress. And then of course often comes the stress associated with debt, whereby we borrow to make up our short-falls, or simply because we believe we can make the repayments. Debt grows sometimes out of necessity, and yet debt is always easy to acquire in the present, but hard to leave behind in the future.

Your spending habits can lead to unprecedented stress and clutter, and often provide momentary (and forgettable) pleasure that will be resented in the event of financial catastrophe.

Life throws us many events we have no control over, but we don't have to live in fear of them and thus not enjoy our money or our lives. It's just about redirecting money to more meaningful endeavours, and questioning your current spending habits.

First, it might be helpful to try and understand the root cause of your bad spending habits, to then know how to change things. This is somewhat easier said than done and there are many influencers in our lives that lead to excess spending. **Ryan T. Howell of Psychology Today discusses the findings of a study on why people overspend [13]; "...materialists are more likely to be compulsive buyers (although not all compulsive buyers are necessarily materialists) because they don't manage their credit as well as general consumers, believe that purchases will transform their lives, and buy for emotional relief".**

That isn't really a surprising statement, with advertising preying on human desires and emotions to instil that need to consume. So the combination of this, mixed with our sometimes challenging day-to-day life, creates willing, impulsive and repeat consumers out of us.

But it goes beyond your general vulnerability as an aspirational spender, with another important factor being your upbringing, whereby growing up around a multiplicity of things and the security of your parents money management can have a mixed impact on how you live; this is certainly true in my experience, but of course the opposite, having very little growing up, will also shape your attitude to consumerism in a certain way. You might develop a passionate work ethic, having had a lot or conversely very little, and yet, you make frivolous spending decisions often. Maybe you have a well-paid or difficult job and you feel justified in enjoying those earnings. You feel like it's okay to spend what money you have each month because you gave so much time in the pursuit of it, so why would you leave it building up in a bank account where you might never get to enjoy it?

Furthermore, your approach to acquiring and keeping things can be the result of growing up with an abundance of material possessions, meaning you come to expect a life full of things; it's your normality and you simply don't know how to live in a different more sustainable manner. And so as you head into adulthood you might try to maintain the situation and retain the sense of security it brings you via excessive and impulsive spending habits, even when your circumstances might no longer support this.

Some of us are simply easily attracted to items when we visit shops online or in person. We are sometimes just susceptible to something that looks new, shiny and useful, especially when we feel like we want to 'treat' ourselves. This isn't necessarily a result of seeking emotional relief although it could be a reaction to boredom, a problem we try to fix by acquiring some new goody that will bring some brief excitement to our day.

It's worth noting that many of the impulse spending choices we make each day, do arise out of our basic human needs. For example, you are walking to work first thing in the morning, and you realize you feel thirsty. You didn't bring water and you know there's a coffee-shop right near your work so you'll just head in and grab one, and that will fix your thirst. But that basic human need has been warped and confused over time; your mind is pushing you to get a coffee because you like it, maybe you're even a little bit addicted to it. Realistically you know you should just grab some tap water before you leave home each day, or wait until you get to work to make a free drink. But those options just aren't as appealing as you're favourite coffee shop drink. But if you buy that coffee every day for a month, each time you walk to work without a drink on your person, that small daily price adds up to a major expense.

Other times our approach to spending goes beyond all the above logical reasons, and is actually linked to our intrinsic self-esteem, or lack of, in that we buy lots of things that are visible to our peers, because we feel the need to match or compete with them e.g. buying the latest fashions or upgrading your car. We lack self-confidence and find that it can be boosted by accruing things and adding them to our image. And yet the buzz is short-lived, as these things previously imbued with special confidence-boosting abilities, eventually wither and die in your opinion. That new outfit that 6 months ago made you feel like the most attractive person in the room, or that new gadget that impressed your friends, just doesn't seem as shiny over time. Our commercialized world relies upon us tiring of our things, which we regularly do, which leads to our repeat consumption. By creating new things all the time, offering just a mildly differentiated version, we are invited to have things, use them, but never make a commitment to them.

No matter the reasoning underpinning our relationship to acquiring things, the more important consideration should be the wider impact of our own choices as individual consumers. There was once a simpler world which when infiltrated by the impenetrable force of capitalism was forever altered. Now and in the future, our very existence on this planet is in threat, due to a culture of excess and wastefulness. But we can choose to not be influenced by our culture and our peers, and we can step away from the manipulation of advertising and social media, recognize the damaging effect it has upon us, and realize that our true worth goes beyond what we own.

We can take stock of what does bring us deep and lasting joy within our lives, and see where a healthier relationship to the paper in our wallets can develop.

Previously, you briefly analysed your relationship with obtaining and keeping things, earlier in the book, in order to ease you through the stage of letting go of clutter. But now it's time to place your entire focus on what might feel like quite a difficult phase, confronting the topic of money; how much you have, how much you owe, how much you'd like to have, and how to sort out financial messes.

STEP 1:
UNDERSTAND YOUR FINANCIAL SITUATION

1. Look at your latest monthly bank statement. Highlight different figures or make a note of them.
- Note what kind of expense they relate to (fixed or changeable).
- Of course you might have made random cash purchases in the month, which you might not remember all of, but try to recall as many as possible, or refer to receipts.

2. Label which amounts correspond to different categories such as utilities, necessities, travel, food, eating out, going out, clothing and miscellaneous.
- Add up the amounts corresponding to each category. This is to establish the reality of where your money is spent, versus the common quote of 'I don't know where my money goes!'.

- Observe how many of the things you label as necessities are actually integral to your daily life.
- Note how many times in that month you did food shopping.
- Is it sporadic and done in short, small trips at different stores, or do you actually write a list of what you need and try to buy it all at once, keeping to a budget?

3. When you have your final amounts for that month, whilst they may be partially estimated, consider if the findings on what you spend on those things not considered a necessity are at all surprising.
- Now also list how much you put into savings each month, as well as how much you pay off of your debts.

4. Pay attention to the expenses that you view as non-essential or optional. Then look at your monthly debt repayments.
- Are you spending more on random, possibly non-essential items, than you are on your debt repayments?
- Add up the amounts you spent on these non-essential items including what you spend on monthly outings and 'treat's, and ask, is it possible that you could take this amount, each month, and add it onto your debt repayments?
- If you were to add this amount to your repayments, how long would it take to clear your debts?
- If you aren't in debt, consider how much this money would add to your savings. Savings are usually much more motivating because you are building something for a future goal or dream as opposed to parting with your money forever, into the black hole of debt.

The key here is that by removing impulse temptation from the now, you will focus on paying off the debts your past temptations might have contributed to. Or, you could build a savings account faster and reach a particular goal sooner.

STEP 2:
OUTLINE YOUR FINANCIAL GOALS

You've looked at the raw data, and you cannot argue with your spending behaviour. But maybe you're still justifying expenses that some might view as non-essential, and maybe distancing yourself from your goals.

An article by Ryan T. Howell on his blog, Beyond the Purchase, remarked on research findings which suggest that saving can actually produce happier feelings compared to spending, and the key to this is having an '...anticipatory vision', essentially a goal for why you are saving [14]. This step focuses on outlining the way you want your money to work for you versus how it currently isn't.

You might have debts, fixed outgoings, and maybe not a high income, but you might also feel motivated to improve the situation where possible. Setting a goal for either clearing a debt, to then afford a trip of a life-time, or some other meaningful financial outcome, is surely the thing that will motivate you to see through the changes.

ANALYSE YOUR CURRENT FINANCIAL STATE:

1. How is your income currently serving your overall purpose and life goals?
2. Is it merely meeting your everyday costs?
3. Do your everyday costs feel out-of-control and overwhelming?
4. Are you accurately measuring your costs as needs versus wants?
5. Is there a specific goal you want to achieve but feel like you can't the way things are financially?
6. Outline these goals, big or small, what they mean to you and when you want to achieve them.

You might feel the need to change your habits radically to increase the rate at which you reach your financial goals. Firstly, before we consider the habits that can help save you money by discouraging spending, we must prepare a mindset that is focused on sticking to our goals.

FORMING THE MINDSET FOR CLEARING DEBT (OR SAVING UP):

1.Embrace the concept of delayed gratification.
- We have these future goals and aims but we then live very much in the present with our money. Money comes in and goes out, in this endless cycle of gaining and losing. Sometimes that's because we have bills to pay and no matter what, they come like clockwork every month. But we still try to acquire things and experiences with relatively limited funds, and end up adding to that cycle.
- This leads to an overall dissatisfaction, as we try to have it all, right now. But when we get a bit more tight with our spending in the present, we do so with a view to delaying our gratification to some future point where we can finally achieve the goal that we had previously felt we never could.
- When we live purely in the now, we use the unpredictable transience of life as the justification for debt. We decide that debt is the only way we can fulfil our dreams like going on an exotic holiday. But if you don't get hit by the proverbial bus, you may have seized the day but you now get to pay for it every month, eventually giving much more away through borrowing than what you could have saved with some patience.

2. Consider the future regret you might experience if you continue to spend your money with abandon.
- From personal experience, I view money I spent in the past as money that I could really do with now. I bring my past spending decisions into the present and it makes me feel regretful. I know that had I saved that money up it would be benefiting me today.
- When you next neglect saving in favour of achieving instant spending gratification, think, how much could you one day regret the cumulative amount of money that your impulse spending will amount to.

- If you believe that you can only find amusement in spending, it's your main hobby and that your future isn't decided by what's in your bank account, its based on daily gratification, then you need to remind yourself why you are doing the cleanse.
- You cannot untie your spending habits from their relationship to stress, and so you have to confront them.
- You have to seek out other ways of finding joy, and you know this, because you want a more sustainable path to calm and inner fulfilment.

3. Expect that you might feel buried by debt, and tired by the thought of a future spent clearing it, but realize you are now on the right path toward never feeling this stressed again.

- You made mistakes in the past, some small and minor, others more memorably impulsive. But your past isn't a determination of your future from now on. If you really knuckle down on your habits, you have the power to change things.
- Accept that money isn't the root of all your stresses, nor is having it abundance going to make life easier and happier forever. But by changing your spending habits, you can end up feeling more able to cope with the times that usually bring the most stress: each time a bill is paid, or each time you have to meet an unexpected expense, because you will be making your money, however much you have, work for your needs.

Appreciate that the process of clearing debt or saving up isn't going to be a short-cut to happiness. In fact for a while you might feel deprived because you are longer responding to impulse thinking and serving your immediate wants. You might end up feeling more bored than ever or more tempted to spend, because you suddenly can't.

That is where the next step comes in. It will suggest some daily habits and thought patterns that you can use to change your relationship with money, today.

STEP 3:
CREATING SPENDING HABITS THAT EASE FINANCIAL STRAIN

These tips are simple things to bring into your mindset of spending, that can have a positive impact on your bank balance. You need to step out of the spend and guilt cycle, and take an active approach every day to do this, until these thoughts turn into habits. **A 2009 study disputed previous research which suggested it took only 21 days to form a new habit, finding that 66 days was a more realistic time-frame [15];** so you could be around two months away from permanently healthier habits, which is a short amount of time of using focused effort versus the long-term benefits.

1. Open some online savings accounts (you can usually do this via your online banking) and use these as virtual piggy-banks.
- Name each account and give it a purpose. My accounts for example are based on RENT, SAVINGS, and DEBITS. This means I can quickly put aside the funds that I want to save, and that I need to save for my fixed expenses, as soon as money comes in.
- It allows me to see at a quick glance exactly where I am at with my saving and spending goals, and of course, means I don't accidentally spend my rent.

2. Get to recognize your common triggers for spending.
- What time of the day do you find yourself thinking about buying something? Could you use this time to do your **'5-minute Blitz'**? Could you read a book, watch a film or switch off your devices to remove temptation?
- Where are the places you go where you spend the most? If you have to visit these places, could you visit them less, or only visit them with an express purpose, list and budget?
- Do your moods often lead you to random spending? Could you consider writing down your feelings somewhere, talking about them with a friend or family member, instead of just adding things to a shopping cart?

3. Avoid, where possible, the places and activities that lead to spending, like window shopping.

- When you do need to go and buy something, write down a list. At the top of this list write your budget for that shopping trip.
- Tick off each item you pick up to buy, and write down the amount spent.
- This will make the process of shopping much more mindful and make you aware of every thought process that follows you from entering a shop, to leaving. From finding the item you need, to being tempted by random deals, to considering the money you are about to hand-over from your budget, it takes the impulse element away and makes shopping much less fun.
- Shopping is simply spending money in exchange for things which sustain your life, and has only been built up as a positive or fun activity thanks to our societal consumerist conditioning, but you can boil it down to what it really is.

4. Anticipate impulse spending decisions and make provisions for these. Like the earlier example of being thirsty and ending up in a coffee-shop, you can anticipate and prevent this spending by making sure you always have a drink with you.

- Re-use a water bottle, or buy a sports bottle, fill it with your favourite drink, and put in the fridge the night before work (or make a flask of a hot drink instead).
- You could even go so far as to trying different recipes and creations, at home, so that you don't look forward to eating out, or buying a quick coffee, you look forward to the affordability of turning your kitchen into a space of inspiration.
- Apply this idea to other things you end up buying on impulse, not just food and drink.

5. Consider not carrying debit or credit cards with you when you are headed to the places that usually result in you spending.

- You could adopt the cash method which I use, whereby I withdraw my weekly spending budget in cash on payday, and then I am confronted with the reality of stretching that money.
- It could seem like a stressful thing to do, that doesn't account for unpredictable expenses, but for the most part it helps you stick to your budget, re-think your purchases and strive to find cheaper options for the things you need.
- It makes money more real, not just a set of numbers on a computer screen. It becomes a tangible thing that you can either hand over mindlessly and lose quickly, or use carefully and still have some left come the end of your budgeting period.

6. Each and every time you consider handing over cash, consider the lifetime and purpose of the item you are buying.

- Is it something you need to get through the next week, like food. Or is it merely something you will get and consume within a day. There's nothing wrong with treating yourself but usually you should do this when you have actually already kept to your budget, only then should you reward your wants.
- By doing this you will come to associate your treats with achievement, and this will positively reinforce the behaviour that helps you consistently meet your budgeting goals.

7. If you struggle to differentiate a need from a want, consider constantly reminding yourself of your biggest goal, the one that you can only reach if you are spending carefully.

- If you are in a shop, be thinking of that goal, and consider the money you might be tempted to hand over, as selling time, the time that you will need to regain those funds and get closer to your goals.
- Visualize your financial goal's not just when you are in a shop or when you get paid, or during the times when you are most commonly tempted to spend, but in other times too.

- When you go to bed, and when you wake-up, allow yourself a few brief moments to think of it. Don't live every second for it, but try to have it at the forefront of your mind, because temptation and impulse spending will always try to push it to the very back.
- When we give into our urges and experience the buzz that we long ago created through our excess and emotional spending, our future goals are further squashed and quietened. Thus to prevent your urges surfacing and taking over, your main financial goal has to become your dominant motivation, replacing the promise of instant gratification.

8. Re-think the things you view as treats, or hobbies, and their relationship to your financial goals.
- Going out for a meal at a fancy restaurant, watching the latest cinema release, or of course, going on a shopping trip, at their core, are expensive.
- We view them as treats because we know we can't afford to do them regularly, and yet do we ever question the why of doing them anyway?
- In reality you can create an awesome meal or feast at home, for half the price, or if you just like getting out the house, it can be pretty fun to just fill up a basket with treats from the local supermarket, and go for a picnic. We know this but ultimately we still build up certain treat experiences as the be-all and end-all of our enjoyment in life.
- We often like the idea of someone else creating and providing our entertainment, meaning we give minimal effort, and so we pay over the odds to have this.
- We give in to the ease and speed with which these treats can be had, from getting our dinner cooked by someone we don't know and delivered to our door, to the relative speed of shopping online. We disengage from the process of acquiring our treats and thus distance ourself from their cost over time by chasing convenience.

61

- You might actually be constantly pouring money into treats that have become habitual, even dull, and so your hard-earned money, when allocated for these 'treat's, is not really bringing you happiness.
- Consider looking into different ways you can reward yourself, that are either not associated with spending, or are simply more affordable to do.

The most important thing to take away from the above advice is that we might be habitually doing things which harm us financially and take our consciousness away from our bigger life goals. We may have over time developed spending habits which we don't even recognize as detrimental because we are so tied up in instant gratification as the norm. Put simply, we don't always know that our money situation is bad, or could be improved. Once we sit down and truly look at how we use our money, and marry that with the true goals we hold at our authentic core, we can make positive changes we never even knew were possible.

PART 5:
THIS END IS YOUR BEGINNING

We are nearing the final words of this book, so it's time to consider, how are you feeling at this point?

- Did you tackle each section of the cleanse with patience, honesty and focus?
- Looking at the results of your actions, do you already feel calmer, and has minimalism proven itself as a stress reliever?
- Do you at least feel as if you have offloaded some physical and mental baggage, wiped your slate clean, and created the right environment for reaching your goals?

You have put your mind to some tasks that you may have previously avoided. The ability to confront things even as insignificant as de-cluttering a shelf, is a show of your own strength, and desire for positive change. You needn't feel as if your life is out of your control or that you are going to continue to make it problematic, because you have proven your will and passion for creating a calmer lifestyle.

This might be the final chapter of the book, but it isn't really the end, not of the process of cleansing your life anyway. Each part in this book presented itself as an instructional guide of suggestions. Perhaps some of the suggested steps took on a life of their own and lead you in a direction of personal growth I couldn't have foreseen. Maybe the minimalism life cleanse has acted as a launching pad from which you will continue to enact positive changes.

To aid you in this ongoing process, we are going to leave on some more suggestions for the future. These ideas will help you celebrate your cleansing successes, motivate you to keep going and suggest actionable daily activities that you can build into your minimalist lifestyle. They can also help you to stick to your new positive changes and help prevent you returning to your old ways.

1. Re-evaluate how you react to things around you, and observe whether you are often guilty of procrastination.

- Some of us go through life delaying dealing with certain things, from serious areas such as our health, to simpler things like replying to an email, but in the delay, comes the stress.
- You can only lead a simpler life long-term if you take a pro-active and responsive attitude to what is going around you.
- Try to avoid problems and situations building up which create new areas of stress that you then want to avoid at all costs. You can do this by dealing with everything around you when it happens.
- From something as small as washing the dishes right after you finish eating, to paying a bill as soon it comes, build your routine upon facing things head on.
- Watch out for those times you think the excuse 'I'll deal with that tomorrow', when tomorrow often becomes a week later, or not at all.
- When we actually complete tasks that we might have resisted doing, we feel a massive sense of accomplishment.
- Taking this attitude every day leads us to feeling like more powerful and successful people, if we constantly witness ourselves getting things done, no matter how big or small.

2. When you find yourself struggling with all your new routines, or notice that you are reverting back to old habits, take a moment to sit, and write it down.

- Extract the thoughts and feelings cluttering your mind up, by simply getting them on paper, in a diary or journal.
- Accept that any big life change is going to be a difficult process, because we are the sum of our habits, bad or good.
- We will always remain flawed human beings, prone to mood swings or moments of self-doubt, but we are not bound by these traits in our quest for happiness.
- Habits aren't broken merely in the reading of a guide on how to do so, it comes from time, effort, and not giving up. You can only maintain a new habit or leave behind an old one, by giving yourself momentary breaks to express, without shame, your anxieties and fears.

- If the journey of change becomes too overwhelming, without breathing space in which you can remind yourself of the reasons you started, then it is doomed to fail.
- By having an outlet to express the more difficult moments, we can acknowledge our feelings without wallowing in them, or feeling defeated by them.

3. Try to cultivate a purposeful daily routine where you are able to deal with the things you used to ignore or let build-up, whilst also enjoying life.

- In the past, before creating spaces in your home uniquely related to different areas of your life, such as paying your bills, you probably found things were being neglected or avoided.
- You might have failed to either create a budget, or follow one.
- You may have felt like you had given so much time to your career in a day that you had nothing to left to give loved ones, or yourself.
- Thus it is important to plan your days more mindfully at the beginning of each one.
- Allocating time slots in a day-planner, specifying time limits in which to contribute to completing certain tasks, means you can create a day where you attend to what you need to, *and* what you want to.
- Follow the rule that allocating any time, be it 5 minutes, or 30, to do the things you need to do, is an achievement.
- When you set out to get a major task done in just one day or one hour, you exert a lot of pressure on yourself.
- Small chunks of time spent on the different priorities in our lives can amount to more focused and enthusiastic energy going into our efforts.
- By specifying an amount of time to spend on something, instead of telling ourselves to finish a project, we can make our tasks more manageable and less time consuming, whilst still getting them done successfully.

4. Set aside 20 minutes each week to revisit de-cluttering your home, and consider if you could still remove more items.

- Walk around your home, take notice of fresh clutter build-up or items that still remain and yet have barely got any interest from you in the past month.
- This is really important if you want to not simply keep your space cleansed but also need reminding of why you undertook the process to begin with.
- You shouldn't need to spend too much time each week reviewing your space, once you have done this a few times.
- If you find yourself coming up against the same piles of mess or corners of clutter, consider some new organization methods for these areas.
- For example, maybe add an organizational basket to your hallway entry table, as opposed to leaving it as just a messy table top.
- Consider, some of these re-occurring messy areas could represent areas of your life that you are still avoiding dealing with.
- As said earlier, our homes should represent our hopes and goals, not serve to stop us from dealing with the things that we tend to avoid (and which later bring us stress).

5. Remember to stop and enjoy your home space.

- You worked hard to create an environment that works for your passions, your relaxation and your life goals, instead of inhibiting them, stealing your time and your attention away.
- Sit down and just look at what you yourself created with time and effort; you were able to move your life away from the societal pressure of having things, toward finding a more fulfilling source of inner content and satisfaction.
- Remind yourself of the value that you brought to your home-space by using it more purposefully.
- Spend moments in your newly created spaces and use them for the new theme you assigned to them.
- Actually use that corner chair to sit and read, not look on your phone or laptop.

6. Acknowledge the small moments of success that happen every day.

- Whilst the life cleanse was about embracing moments of big change, going forward you need to learn to appreciate the small victories that every day can bring, even a bad day.
- It's a success to get out of the house on-time for work, to get there in one-piece, to tick some tasks off your to-do list, and to resist spending temptation at lunch-time.
- It's worth celebrating a day where you smiled or laughed at least once, or where you made someone else smile.
- A life built on simpler pleasures and an appreciation of the quieter, supposedly more mundane moments, helps us stop chasing pleasure and fulfilment via consumerism and technological escapism.

7. Celebrate the big moments also.

- Don't underestimate the power of patting yourself on the back when you hit life milestones or complete phases of the cleanse.
- Maybe you finally cleared a big debt, or feel like your home de-clutter is over forever, but don't be afraid to share these successes with people around you.
- Share these changes with your friends and families, and encourage them to make similar minimalist adjustments if you believe it will positively influence their life.
- Being a source of inspiration for people, isn't the same as bragging.

CONCLUDING ON THE CLEANSE

The fundamentals of cleansing your life are more than just the acts put forward in this book. Being calm and more fulfilled, is a journey, and an ongoing challenge. I don't believe that de-cluttering is an automatic shortcut to happiness, but I do believe that the ideas put forth in the book set out achievable actions which lead you in the right direction, and the right direction will mean something different to everyone. From financial stability, to simply having an easier cleaning routine, right up to the height of completely starting your life over; wiping the previous slate, addressing the clutter, physical, technological, financial, and reaffirming your life verve. With your new slate, you can address the other areas of your life, from mental health, to physical health, to your family and relationships.

Deriving meaning from minimalist principles to become a calmer person, goes beyond the words you have followed in this book. But hopefully it has inspired you, and made you feel empowered to change your life and the world, for the better. Basically, I hope this has been a good place to start.

If you enjoyed reading **Minimalism: Cleanse your life, Become a calmer person**, *please share it with someone you think it could benefit. I'd love you come and chat over email, and send a message to nomaderhowfar@gmail.com to let me know how this book helped you in your life, or if you have any further questions or need for guidance. If you found this book truly helped you, please take a moment to help me, by leaving a review of your thoughts at the end.*

ACKNOWLEDGEMENTS

It might say my name as the author of this book, but I haven't achieved this life-long goal alone.

The fact that this book is now able to be read across the world, is not simply due to me finally knuckling down and creating something. I might have formed and built the ideas within this book, but my partner Taran encouraged me to perfect them. He is the one responsible for this even becoming an actual book, as he aided me with the technical side, a part I have no patience for, truly being a bull in a china-shop when there are buttons and computer programs involved. I might have sat and typed all these words out for hours on end, but it was my mother Janet who helped me edit it, sending through a long email of detailed suggestions. She has no editing background but she certainly knows her spelling and grammar.

On a deeper level, the people around me, including my partner and my mother, have helped create the person who was open to the idea of minimalism, who was able to embrace a new way of life, and eventually discover her calling. I thank them and all the other people closest to me for supporting me on my own life cleanse and adoption of minimalism, and who continue to support my devotion to this lifestyle. I also appreciate my friends and family who relentlessly read my blog posts at nomaderhowfar.com and never appear bored by my ramblings, even if they are. I know that they are the ones who have given me confidence in my own words, my ability to relate to my readers and made writing this e-book a passion project, not an exercise in conquering self-doubt.

I feel content beyond measure that you made the choice to give a small amount of money, out of your own pocket, to support this book and thus, the idea of minimalism. The life cleanse can be a self-centred process, but the goals behind it relate closely to the selfless causes we as humans cannot ignore any-more. I believe in our power to turn things around in this world, and know that the dominant ideology of mindless consumption will have some steadfast opposition, soon enough.

Foot Notes

1. Parker-Pope, T. (2008). *A clutter too deep for mere bins and shelves.* [online] Nytimes.com. Available at: http://www.nytimes.com/2008/01/01/health/01well.html?_r=0 [Accessed 22 Apr. 2016].

2. Thieda, K. (2013). *Is Your Loved One Hoarding?.* [online] Psychology Today. Available at: https://www.psychologytoday.com/blog/partnering-in-mental-health/201308/is-your-loved-one-hoarding [Accessed 22 Apr. 2016].

3. Doland, E. (2011). *Scientists find physical clutter negatively affects your ability to focus, process information.* [online] Unclutterer. Available at: https://unclutterer.com/2011/03/29/scientists-find-physical-clutter-negatively-affects-your-ability-to-focus-process-information/ [Accessed 22 Apr. 2016].

4. Kennedy, S. (2016). *Richest 1% Now Wealthier Than the Rest of the World, Oxfam Says.* [online] Bloomberg. Available at: http://www.bloomberg.com/news/articles/2016-01-18/richest-1-now-wealthier-than-the-rest-of-the-world-oxfam-says [Accessed 22 Apr. 2016].

5. Taylor, S. (2012). *The Madness of Materialism.* [online] Psychology Today. Available at: https://www.psychologytoday.com/blog/out-the-darkness/201203/the-madness-materialism [Accessed 22 Apr. 2016].

6. McLeod, S. (2007). *Maslow's Hierarchy of Needs.* [online] Simply Psychology. Available at: http://www.simplypsychology.org/maslow.html [Accessed 22 Apr. 2016].

7. Fontinelle, A. (2013). *American Dream Definition* [online] Investopedia. Available at: http://www.investopedia.com/terms/a/american-dream.asp [Accessed 22 Apr. 2016].

8. Britannica.com. (2016). *postmaterialism -- Britannica Online Encyclopedia.* [online] Available at: http://www.britannica.com/print/article/1286234. [Accessed 22 Apr. 2016]. Further reading: Nelson, E. (2013). *ARE YOU A POST MATERIALIST?.* [online] Ellis Nelson. Available at: https://ellisnelson.com/2013/01/03/are-you-a-post-materialist/. [Accessed 22 Apr. 2016].

9. Jasiewicz, I. (2010) *The Real Mad Men behind the 60's Ad Revolution.* [online] Newsweek. [online] Available at: http://www.newsweek.com/real-mad-men-behind-60s-ad-revolution-74351 [Accessed 22 Apr. 2016].

10. Nyu.edu. (2016). *History of Television - Mitchell Stephens.* [online] Available at: https://www.nyu.edu/classes/stephens/History%20of%20Television%20page.htm [Accessed 22 Apr. 2016].

11. Davidow, B. (2012). *Exploiting the Neuroscience of Internet Addiction.* [online] The Atlantic. Available at: http://www.theatlantic.com/health/archive/2012/07/exploiting-the-neuroscience-of-internet-addiction/259820/ [Accessed 22 Apr. 2016].

12. Anxiety UK. (2012). *Anxiety UK study finds technology can increase anxiety - Anxiety UK.* [online] Available at: https://www.anxietyuk.org.uk/news/for-some-with-anxiety-technology-can-increase-anxiety/ [Accessed 22 Apr. 2016].

13. Howell, R.T. (2013). *What Can Be Done to Help With Compulsive Spending Habits?.* [online] Psychology Today. Available at: https://www.psychologytoday.com/blog/cant-buy-happiness/201308/what-can-be-done-help-compulsive-spending-habits [Accessed 22 Apr. 2016].

14. Howell, R.T. (2014). *The Psychology of Money | Beyond The Purchase Blog.* [online] Available at: http://www.beyondthepurchase.org/blog/08/train-your-brain-to-spend-smarter-a-chat-with-beyondthepurchase-org/ [Accessed 22 Apr. 2016].

15. Dean, S. (2015). *Here's how long it takes to break a habit, according to science.* [online] Science Alert. Available at: http://www.sciencealert.com/here-s-how-long-it-takes-to-break-a-habit-according-to-science [Accessed 22 Apr. 2016].

Made in the USA
San Bernardino, CA
20 January 2018